LOFT STYLE

ARCHITECTURE & DESIGN LIBRARY

LOFT STYLE

Jessica Tolliver

FRIEDMAN/FAIRFAX

A FRIEDMAN/FAIRFAX BOOK

© 2002 by Michael Friedman Publishing Group, Inc.

Please visit our website: www.metrobooks.com

Library of Congress Cataloging-in-Publication Data

Tolliver, Jessica.
  Loft style / [Jessica Tolliver].
      p.cm. -- (Architecture and design library)
  Includes bibliographical references and index.
  ISBN 1-58663-305-8
  1. Lofts. I. Title. II. Series.

NK2117.L63 T65 2002
729--dc21

                            2001050149

Editor: Hallie Einhorn
Art Director: Kevin Ullrich
Designer: Orit Mardkha-Tenzer
Photography Editor: Paquita Bass
Production Manager: Michael Vagnetti

Color separations by Colourscan
Printed in China by C S Graphics Shanghai Co., Ltd.

1 3 5 7 9 10 8 6 4 2

Distributed by Sterling Publishing Company, Inc.
387 Park Avenue South
New York, NY 10016
Distributed in Canada by Sterling Publishing
Canadian Manda Group
One Atlantic Avenue, Suite 105
Toronto, Ontario, Canada M6K 3E7
Distributed in Australia by
Capricorn Link (Australia) Pty, Ltd.
P.O. Box 704, Windsor, NSW 2756 Australia

Love and thanks to Josie, who inspired me to follow a dream,
and to Nate, who assured me that I would succeed.

Contents

INTRODUCTION

Sunny. Spacious. Stylish. Lofts appeal to many urban residents as the ideal living situation. Characterized by sprawling floor plans and enormous windows, they stand in sharp contrast to the claustrophobic apartments in which many city dwellers live. However, lofts attracted their first residents—the artists of New York City in the 1950s—for a far more fundamental reason. Economics.

In search of affordable housing, some resourceful pioneers discovered vacant garment factories and print shops in downtown Manhattan. With brick walls, concrete floors, and exposed ductwork, these vast industrial spaces were devoid of domestic comforts; many didn't even have running water or effective heating. The expansive floor plans and huge freight elevators, however, were able to accommodate the artists' large canvases and sculptures, and the natural light pouring in through the oversize windows was ideal for painting and sculpting. Plus, the spaces were inexpensive and available.

Artists promptly started to move in, taking over the former factories and workshops for both work and residential purposes. Even though they needed to conceal their activities from landlords and city officials (the industrial spaces were not yet zoned for residential use), the new occupants gradually began to add the rudiments of modern living, albeit in rather unconventional, matter-of-fact ways. Tubs and showers were installed in the middle of floors, and kitchen sinks were haphazardly plugged into empty strips of wall. Surreptitiously, the artists tapped into public utilities, including water, gas, and electricity. A movement had begun.

In the decades that have passed since those humble beginnings, people all over the world have come to embrace loft-style living. Drenched in sunshine and blessed with a luxurious amount of space, lofts offer a welcome alternative to the confinement of most urban residences. And those industrial details—from concrete columns to exposed metal pipes—are now regarded as the height of style. In increasing numbers, urban residents are moving into a wide variety of commercial spaces, including former garment factories, vacant schools and office buildings, and abandoned warehouses.

OPPOSITE: *This soaring, sun-filled loft offers all the comforts of home. The open floor plan not only maximizes the use of space, but also creates the backdrop for a casual, relaxed way of life.*

While the level of decor and amenities has risen since the early days, current loft dwellers are maintaining the qualities that first drew them to these spaces. Almost all the public rooms of the home—the living and dining areas, the kitchen, and the foyer—occupy a single enormous space. Even areas usually considered private, such as bedrooms and baths, may be left open to their surroundings. The result is a flowing, light-filled residence that encourages the more casual lifestyle prevalent today. Family members can eat dinner in shifts at the kitchen counter, guests may pitch in with meal preparation, and children are definitely both seen and heard.

Even city officials, who once knocked on loft doors late at night in an effort to ferret out illegal residents, value the resurgence that the loft movement has brought to urban centers. No longer low-budget accommodations, many lofts now house the upper crust of society. And as homeowners turn their lofts into upscale enclaves, developers are similarly transforming the surrounding areas into fashionable destinations. All over the world, neighborhoods that stood deserted and destitute for years are now teeming with swanky shops and cafés. In New York, for example, the loft-filled areas of SoHo and TriBeCa have become two of the city's most desirable locales. Art galleries, pricey restaurants, and chain stores now line the once forlorn streets. As a result, artists and others on tight budgets, forced out by prohibitive prices, are moving across the rivers to Brooklyn, Queens, and New Jersey in an effort to locate untouched lofts.

In rapid fashion, the loft movement is similarly changing the face of urban centers across the United States—Chicago, Detroit, and Seattle—and the world—London, Prague, and Madrid. The impact of the loft on housing reaches far beyond city boundaries, though. Once a revolutionary concept for living, the loft includes architectural features that can now be found in homes on just about any suburban street in America.

Around the time that artists first started moving into lofts, a new casual lifestyle was emerging in the United States. Americans, then accustomed to houses divided into several single-purpose rooms, were beginning to demand homes that would allow them to spend time together—not keep them sequestered based on their activities. The large, open floor plan of a loft lends itself perfectly to that way of life, and Americans soon took notice. (At the same time, the modernists were starting to design homes that would meet those same needs.)

The open layout that once defined the loft as a brand-new concept for living can now be found in every style of home. Today, new houses—even those lining suburban streets—usually feature a great room that merges the living room, dining room, and kitchen into one expansive space. And owners of old homes—from historic town houses to stately Colonials—are knocking down walls to create wide-open spaces out of several tiny rooms. While these open floor plans rarely replicate the scale of a loft, they do mimic the free-flowing feeling.

Similarly, the industrial materials found in lofts are becoming increasingly common in typical homes. The pages of any decorating magazine picture concrete floors and countertops, walls of exposed brick, and large exposed ceiling beams. In suburban homes everywhere, kitchens include stainless steel refrigerators and ranges, while baths feature plumbing fixtures with chrome fittings and deliberately exposed piping. Decades ago, the general population gaped at the use of such industrial materials in the home; most now regard them as a mark of true style. Plus, homeowners have come to realize the wisdom of installing materials designed to withstand the harshest daily activities—even those of a factory.

Just as they have influenced other aspects of culture, artists initiated the movement to adapt lofts for residential living. But in their search for affordable housing, they tapped into a far more complex human desire. Whether in the city or the suburbs, people want their residences to function as comfortable and uplifting retreats. For many, the hallmarks of urban lofts—space, sunlight, and a casual layout—fulfill this need. And, luckily, each of these qualities can be adapted for almost any living situation.

ABOVE: *A restrained use of furnishings helps maintain the openness of this loft without sacrificing comfort. The simple lines of the pieces contribute to the space's uncluttered look.*

LEFT: *With its open-plan layout, ultrahigh ceilings, and almost uninterrupted expanse of floor, this residence is the epitome of loft design. Despite its vast size, the space feels hospitable because "rooms" have been created with the help of strategic furniture arrangements and such architectural features as columns and a fireplace.*

ABOVE: *In one corner, a splash of yellow, a pair of lipstick red chairs, and a piece of artwork create an intimate spot for a chat à deux. The contrast of the colors, the sculptural lines of the chairs, and the whimsical nature of the side table make the area as visually appealing as it is welcoming.*

OPPOSITE: *To cordon off the formal dining room from its surroundings, partial "walls" were created by using enormous fans and steel rails. The oversize scale of the two fans honors the industrial origins of the loft.*

RIGHT: *A perforated screen effectively sections off a bedroom. Though the lines of the furniture are simple and the accessories minimal, an element of warmth permeates the space thanks to the rich hues of the rug and the sunshine streaming through the skylight.*

CHAPTER ONE

THE CANVAS

The artists who first took up residence in urban lofts found more than just the cheap rent appealing. In these former factories and workshops, creative spirits saw potential homes unlike any they—or anyone else—had ever known. Far from being put off by the industrial aesthetic, the pioneering artists were attracted to the style.

By definition, lofts are vast, open spaces. Sprawling floor plans stretch from front wall to back, side to side, dwarfing many other homes—particularly urban ones—in size. Composed of—at least originally—one expansive room, these renovated commercial spaces speak to a freedom of movement and a sense of fluidity.

The benefits of such spacious areas are certainly practical. Artists, of course, prize lofts for their ability to comfortably accommodate their creative endeavors. But for residents of the world's busiest cities, the appeal is far greater; after all, the vast landscapes of lofts provide a reprieve from the crowded streets and tiny spaces that are typical of urban centers.

The enormous floor plans were originally designed to accommodate the workings of large-scale factories. But the expansive open layout is not the only architectural element that loft dwellers have inherited from the days in which their residences served as workshops. Ceilings, for instance, are extremely high—often reaching twenty feet (6m) or higher—a trait initially designed to allow room for the large machinery inhabiting the factories. Along exterior walls, vast windows soar from close to the floor all the way to the ceiling, providing much of the illumination and ventilation for the once bustling workrooms. To supplement ventilation and to garner even more sunlight, lofts located on the top floors of buildings often boast several large, operable skylights. As a result, natural light serves as an important element of the loft's architecture, as integral as the expansive stretches of flooring and the soaring ceilings.

Because the original developers of the factories valued economics over aesthetics, many of a building's structural features, which in most homes are hidden behind plaster or drywall, are left exposed to the

OPPOSITE: *A ventilation duct located in midair brings the scale of this loft down to earth. Juxtaposed against the vertical lines of the huge windows—which echo the Chicago skyscrapers in the distance—the duct injects a graphic element.*

composed of exposed brick, support columns tend to be made of concrete, and floors consist of either concrete or wood planking. Metal and rubber also figure prominently; the former appears as cast-iron plumbing pipes, aluminum window muntins, and industrial-size steel bolts on support beams, to give a few examples, while rubber often manifests itself in electrical wiring and sometimes flooring.

Some final architectural remnants of the loft's hardworking past include extremely large doors and freight elevators, sized to allow for easy transport of the factory's product. Usually faced with steel or aluminum, but sometimes wood, these hefty features were originally designed to withstand the constant banging and crashing that come with heavy-duty manufacturing.

Although the residents of lofts today do not operate printing presses or produce large volumes of clothing like their predecessors did, they do appreciate the aesthetic that their forebears created out of necessity. The sweeping floor plans, seemingly sky-high ceilings, large windows, and industrial-grade materials come together in surroundings that are attractive and impressive. And even though most modern loft dwellers modify their homes to allow for some creature comforts, the most thoughtful ones do so in a manner that maintains the integrity of the industrial setting and honors the heritage of the space.

ABOVE: *Exposed brick walls along with wood floors and ceiling beams fill this loft with warmth. Arches at the windows provide a softening touch.*

OPPOSITE: *Although the walls of this bedroom have been finished with plaster, a glimpse of brick around the window reveals the original architecture of the room. Pipes overhead have been painted white to blend in with the ceiling.*

eye. Bulky columns and piers, spread out across the space to provide support where needed, pierce the landscape of the loft; ceiling beams and vaults are also readily visible.

The usually behind-the-scenes workings of utilities tend to remain in full view, as well. Ventilation ductwork and electrical lines often weave back and forth across the ceiling, while plumbing and heating pipes tend to run up and down corners and along the bottom of walls.

Again, even though these features were left exposed for practical reasons, they contribute to the aesthetic of the loft. Panels to conceal overhead beams, ductwork, and wiring would have resulted in lower ceilings, and wallboard to hide support beams and pipes would have interrupted the flow of space. With the skeleton of a building left on view, the maximum amount of possible living space is visible and available for use.

To stand up to the abuse of working factories, lofts were originally constructed of the hardiest materials available. Hence, walls are usually

OPPOSITE: *To maintain the powerful sense of space and height in this soaring loft, sight lines are left open; the second-story walkway is lined with translucent glass panels, and the staircase is designed with the openness of a ladder. The timeworn demeanor of the timber support beams and columns contrasts with the fine finish of the plaster walls.*

RIGHT: *Steel beams create an industrial-style lattice of sorts, allowing sunshine from the skylights to filter through to the living space below. In order to maximize the play of light and heighten the airy feeling, the walls, steel beams, and overhead fixtures are bathed in white. Even though the steel facing that envelops the pod is new, it takes its cue from the loft's past life as a commercial space.*

OPPOSITE and RIGHT: *Sleek materials— from glass to metal to smooth white plaster— abound in this loft, giving it a high-style look. Only the bulky ventilation duct suspended beneath the ceiling reveals the hard-working history of the space. Notice how the gleaming stainless steel cabinets and appliances in the kitchen tie in with the less refined metal duct.*

ABOVE: *Despite the sophisticated furnishings in this loft, the nicks and blemishes of the concrete ceiling celebrate the space's industrial roots. An expanse of exposed brick by the stairs also contrasts with the fine elements that are scattered throughout the loft.*

OPPOSITE: *On the second floor, concrete continues to have a strong presence. Because the ceiling is not concealed behind a layer of plaster, electrical wiring is visible overhead.*

OPPOSITE: *True to loft style, some of the functional architectural elements of this building are left exposed, including a massive column. In addition to its primary role of providing structural support, the column helps define the distinct areas of the loft.*

ABOVE: *Although a couple of walls have been introduced to break up the space a bit, a powerful sense of openness prevails. While these additions have a crisp look, the raw quality of the loft's first life continues to manifest itself in the ceiling and the exterior wall.*

CHAPTER TWO

LIGHT

Bountiful light ranks as one of the primary appeals of loft living. After all, a generous dose of sunshine brings welcome relief from the often dreary confines of city living. Outfitted with windows that sail from wall to wall and floor to ceiling, lofts offer bright and sunny surroundings—a rare treat in an urban environment.

Adapting these huge industrial spaces to residential living can put that treasured natural light at risk, though. Domestic necessities such as window coverings to ensure privacy, walls to cordon off bedrooms and baths, and banks of kitchen cabinets to house cooking implements often come with the unwanted effect of obstructing prized sunshine. Thus, when retrofitting lofts to serve as homes, owners and designers must take great care to retain as much natural light as possible.

Not surprisingly, the creative spirits that reside in urban lofts have devised countless solutions for maximizing natural light. Take, for instance, the varied approaches to window treatments. Although many homeowners deem it necessary to block the view from neighboring buildings, they adopt measures to do so without sacrificing sunlight. One approach is to incorporate frosted glass windows beneath a row of clear panes. The frosted glass obscures inward views of the area where activity actually takes place yet still admits outside light; meanwhile, the clear glass units above give residents glimpses of the cityscape while ushering in unhampered sunshine. For loft dwellers who don't want frosted glass to block their own views permanently, windows made of glass that changes from clear to opaque at the flip of a switch are now available. Sheer curtains provide a less high-tech option; plus, the breezy diaphanous fabric offers a softening counterpoint to the many hard surfaces of a loft. In lofts that occupy the top floor of a building, skylights are favored for inviting in additional sunshine.

Interior walls present another obstacle to the free flow of light. Although most loft dwellers need to create at least a couple of private spaces—a bedroom or two, a bath, and maybe a study—few resort to building typical walls. Partial walls, which often reach eight to ten feet (2.4 to 3m) high instead of all the way to the ceiling, permit the passage

OPPOSITE: *Mounted above a dining table, sleek chrome light fixtures create a sense of drama. A translucent partition, reminiscent of a Japanese shoji screen, shields the view of the adjacent kitchen but allows subtle light to enter the room.*

of light between the different areas while still providing sufficient privacy. Similarly, walls crafted of such translucent but view-obscuring materials as glass block, frosted glass, and reeded plastic help to achieve light-filled interiors.

No matter how successful a loft dweller's efforts at making the most of natural light, artificial sources are also necessary. After all, the sun doesn't shine all day, and even during daylight hours those parts of a loft located farthest away from the windows could use some help. The oversize scale of this type of residence, however, requires a strategic approach to lighting; a couple of table lamps will do little justice to the architecture of a loft.

When designing a lighting plan, the goal is to arrange fixtures in such a way as to create what professionals refer to as layers of light. The first step toward accomplishing this effect is to illuminate the space with an overall brightness—referred to as ambient light—that appears as natural as possible. For a loft, the choice is often recessed fixtures or strip lighting; the former is favored for its unobtrusive quality while the latter is embraced for its ability to blend with the industrial surroundings. Next, fixtures that illuminate a specific area or work space—such as a dining table or a kitchen counter—are incorporated. These helpful fixtures are appropriately referred to as task lighting. When situated properly, task lighting not only serves the practical purpose of shedding light on a desktop or cutting board, but also offers the opportunity to create zones of intimacy in a large space. Finally, accent lighting—which provides decoration either on its own or by calling attention to artwork—is added.

Task and accent lighting provide great outlets for creativity. A resourceful homeowner, for instance, might hang a large aluminum pendant salvaged from an old elementary school over the dining table. Many floor and table lamps, as well as wall sconces, are so sculptural that they stand as works of art in and of themselves. As an alternative, carefully placed pin lights along an angled wall can serve as an eye-catching collage.

In fact, there are a number of ways to incorporate accent lighting into the very architecture of a loft. Consider, for example, a floor with a patch of glass block at its center; illuminated from beneath by an artificial source, the glass block brings subtle brightness to the area and creates a focal point. On an interior wall, a false window can be backlit with artificial light to create the illusion of natural brightness.

Last but not least, the deft use of color can serve as a complement to both natural and artificial light. For many, white is the preferred choice, as it reflects light. However, a splash of a more vivid hue, such as orange or pink, brings a sense of energy and vitality to even the dullest of days.

OPPOSITE: *In this kitchen, a vaulted ceiling composed almost entirely of glass barely interrupts the line of the brick exterior wall. For the lucky chef, the result is a sun-drenched work space.*

LEFT: *Though actually quite narrow, this hallway appears bright and fluid thanks to the curved, translucent wall on the right. To further enhance the open feeling, both walls reach only partway to the ceiling.*

OPPOSITE: *Light pours into the dining area both through and over the translucent partition. Removed from the surrounding areas but not completely cut off, the space enjoys a hint of formality without feeling stuffy or confined.*

TOP and BOTTOM: *When important company arrives, steel doors can be slid into place to partially conceal the view of this eat-in kitchen. For day-to-day activity, they are left open so that the interior space can benefit from the windows on the other side of the hall. A glass screen ensures that some amount of natural light reaches the kitchen during daytime hours.*

ABOVE: *When natural light isn't enough, recessed fixtures step in to illuminate the kitchen. A large pass-through not only makes serving meals easier, but also promotes the flow of light.*

OPPOSITE: *Two large sliding glass doors seem to eliminate the boundary between indoors and out. In the distance, recessed lighting peeks out from a floating panel suspended just beneath the ceiling.*

RIGHT: *Doors featuring full-length glass panels team up with floor-to-ceiling windows to unify a terrace with the interior living space. Whether indoors or out, occupants can view a wide swatch of sky, deep in the heart of the city.*

LEFT: *The abundance of sunshine that can pour into a loft proves true the old adage that it's possible to have "too much of a good thing." Here, white venetian blinds cut down on the glare without completely blocking the light. Sleek and minimalist, the window treatments maintain the clean look of the space.*

A B O V E : *Two interior windows allow light to flow freely between a bedroom and the adjacent living space. Blinds or shades could be installed to provide privacy when desired.*

OPPOSITE: *A greenhouse design stretches along one end of a loft, allowing in the maximum amount of sunlight. A small café table is situated to catch the rays.*

RIGHT: *As glamorous as can be, this staircase features a glass enclosure and glass steps that seem to float on air. Sunshine from the top floor pours down both flights of stairs and into the interior living space.*

ABOVE: *Frosted panes envelop this sitting area to filter glaring sunlight and ensure privacy. Two clear windows—one of which wraps around the corner—take advantage of the view.*

ABOVE: *Massive glass doors swing into place to divide the sunny sitting area from the adjacent living room while allowing light to pass freely between the two. When open, the large doors are barely noticeable. A row of recessed lights helps to mark the transition between the two spaces and encourages visitors to watch their step.*

OPPOSITE: *A clean line of recessed lights overhead unobtrusively brightens a passageway. When the doors at the far end are open, the lights effectively draw the eye to the windows and stunning view beyond.*

ABOVE: *Several more recessed fixtures are located directly above the dining table, casting a soft glow on meals. To the right, three light-as-a-feather spotlights are as eye-catching as the painting they illuminate.*

CHAPTER THREE

DEFINING SPACE

The sweeping layouts characteristic of lofts provide a refreshing change of scenery from the crowded streets typical of city life. The challenge for loft dwellers, however, is to maintain the feeling of wide-open space while addressing the requirements of modern living. Privacy must be created for sleeping, bathing, and working areas without making these spaces seem closed off. And distinct zones for cooking, eating, and relaxing within an open floor plan are desirable to achieve a homey feeling. Spaces designated for specific purposes not only function better, but also create a comforting sense of order and intimacy. If not treated properly, the vast landscape of a loft can feel cold and forbidding instead of liberating and welcoming.

Not surprisingly, designers and loft dwellers have devised countless techniques for establishing defined areas without creating a warren of small, single-purpose rooms. These many and varied solutions are as individual as the homeowners themselves.

The most leeway exists with respect to the public zones of the loft—namely the living and dining areas and the kitchen. Because these areas do not require privacy, there is a considerable amount of flexibility when it comes to design options. Something as simple as a low set of shelves can mark the border of a sitting area. Plus, this handy device can serve a dual purpose, providing storage for books or display space for decorative objects. A low wall will also clearly define one end of an activity area without disrupting the visual flow of the room.

Varying the heights of the ceiling and the floor is another method employed by designers to demarcate space. A dropped ceiling located just over the kitchen or a conversation area fosters a sense of intimacy. A dining table elevated two or three steps above the rest of the loft looks and feels dramatic.

Another approach to the challenge of defining space involves changes of color and texture. By using different materials and hues in adjacent activity areas, a sense of distinction can be achieved. For instance, a dining area could be decked out in wood, while its neighboring kitchen might be sheathed in stainless steel. One wall of a

OPPOSITE: *When the owners of this loft want to block the view of the kitchen from the dining area, a huge screen rolls easily into place. A massive column serves as an additional— more permanent—boundary marker.*

kitchen might be painted bright red to set it apart from the rest of the loft, or a rectangle of sky blue might be situated over the dining table to help distinguish the eating area. A change in flooring materials can also mark the transition from one zone to another. When the front door opens right onto the living space, as tends to be the case in lofts, a patch of gray slate flooring abutting a sea of honey-colored wood planking can create the sense of a foyer. Similarly, a square of colorful linoleum inset into the corner of an otherwise wood floor could help create a children's play area.

Perhaps the simplest technique of all is to artfully arrange furnishings into "rooms." For instance, an overstuffed chair, a side table, and an attractive lamp clustered together lend the appearance of a cozy reading nook. A love seat and a pair of armchairs situated around a coffee table, perhaps with an area rug underneath, beckon family members to gather together and visit. Positioning the furnishings in different activity areas to face away from each other can heighten the sense of definition. A sofa forms a visual boundary when placed with its back to other zones.

For rooms that require privacy, designers and homeowners have adopted a number of different approaches. Most loft dwellers need at least one bedroom and bath, and some may desire a quiet study. While such rooms tend to require boundaries that are more absolute than those of the public areas, they are still designed to maintain the openness that is integral to loft living.

One popular technique is to situate a bedroom on a mezzanine. Located on an upper level, the sleeping quarters rest out of the sight lines of people on the main floor; the space underneath can serve as a study or cozy sitting area. The beauty of a mezzanine as opposed to a traditional second floor is that it allows the majority of the living space below to enjoy the loft's soaring height.

If the bedroom is to reside on the same level as the rest of the living space, curved walls offer ultimate privacy while still appearing fluid and less restrictive than conventional ones. And two walls can be arranged to overlap slightly, blocking the view of the room within while still providing an entrance. The result is a layout that appears more open and flowing than one broken up by traditional walls.

One of the most dramatic measures is to build a completely enclosed room in the middle of the floor plan. Known as a pod, this type of room sometimes includes a ceiling that is quite a bit lower than the one above the surrounding space. Often, designers include windows or walls of textured or frosted glass in the pod so that the contained room does not obstruct the flow of light through the loft.

The design option that offers the most flexibility is the addition of screens or partitions mounted on tracks that can move in and out of position depending on the needs of the moment. Sliding shoji-inspired screens can be used to close off a work area from distractions while still permitting light to enter. Similarly, these devices can be called upon to lend a bedroom privacy while maintaining a light and airy atmosphere. A freestanding partition on casters can also be slid in and out of position according to the desire for privacy.

The possibilities for defining activity areas in the vast setting of a loft are endless. And there is plenty of room for creativity.

OPPOSITE: *Situated to create a sense of privacy—rather than the reality of it—this open set of shelves displays various treasures. Placed on casters, the entire piece can be moved to the side if desired.*

A B O V E   a n d   O P P O S I T E : *A change in levels helps to establish the boundaries of a home office, as does a low wall that wraps around one end of the work space. Sliding wood panels mounted on tracks add further definition while providing a measure of privacy. As a result of the overall design, the different activity areas enjoy a sense of distinction yet continue to reap the benefits of an open floor plan.*

ABOVE, LEFT: *Stretching about three-quarters of the way to the ceiling, a large wall helps to form both a distinct dining area and an upstairs gallery. Painted bright yellow, the divider serves as an intriguing design element, not just a functional device.*

ABOVE, RIGHT: *Upstairs, a recessed niche in the wall makes room for a desk. Topped by a long row of skylights, the gallery feels more like a tree house than a room in an urban home.*

RIGHT: *In this loft, a mezzanine serves two purposes: housing private zones on a separate floor and creating a sense of intimacy in the foyer. A sparely designed spiral staircase links the two levels without visually consuming space.*

LEFT: *The activity areas of this upbeat loft are divided into three levels: an entryway on the first floor, a kitchen and dining area on the second, and sleeping quarters on the third. The low ceiling formed by the mezzanine, along with a row of support columns, imbues the cooking area with a sense of coziness and warmth.*

ABOVE: *Sliding screens cordon off this office when necessary while still allowing the passage of light. Sheer and geometric, the panels lend a decorative flair to both spaces.*

OPPOSITE: *Strategic groupings of furniture create distinct zones in this expansive loft. Sharing the vast open floor plan are a work studio, a living area, and a dining space.*

ABOVE: *At the other end of the loft, a mezzanine hovers over the eat-in kitchen, creating a sense of intimacy. A change in flooring materials also calls attention to the transition between areas.*

ABOVE: *Sometimes architectural features can act as effective room dividers. Here, a freestanding fireplace successfully creates an air of separation between a dining area and a living room while serving as a focal point for the latter.*

A B O V E : *A simple rug clearly delineates the sitting area. An artful arrangement of furnishings further enhances the sense of definition.*

LEFT: *To create privacy for this bedroom, dramatic folding screens can be pulled shut. Mounted on wheels, the massive dividers can easily be maneuvered. Notice how the bold hues of the screens coordinate with the bed and linens.*

RIGHT: *A beam with a textured paint treatment highlights the transition between the sleeping quarters of a bedroom and its private sitting area. The closet on the left provides valuable storage while breaking up the space.*

ABOVE: *In this loft, a partial wall serves as the only boundary between the living room and bedroom. Outfitted with a fireplace, the wall neatly divides the two spaces without confining them.*

OPPOSITE: *A series of shoji-inspired sliding doors can be pulled shut to enclose this dining area for formal meals. The rest of the time, the doors are left open to maintain the spacious and casual feel of the loft.*

CHAPTER FOUR
PERFORMANCE SPACES

When adapting an industrial space for residential use, the two most obvious additions are the kitchen and bath. Today, owners of every sort of home have come to expect an unprecedented level of performance and luxury from what were once considered merely utilitarian rooms—and loft dwellers are no exception.

At first glance, the decadence of a sumptuous kitchen or a pampering bath seems to be at odds with the rough origins of loft living. After all, the first homesteaders of urban lofts introduced baths by merely installing a tub in the living room and created kitchens by plugging a crockpot into the wall. But in keeping with the sophistication of today's interiors, designers have devised numerous strategies for creating sybaritic enclaves that pay homage to the industrial aesthetic.

When selecting materials for the kitchen and the bath, loft dwellers and designers take their cues from classic loft architecture. And many of these materials just happen to be de rigueur for performance spaces in all sorts of homes—not just lofts.

Stainless steel is a perfect example. Homeowners and professional chefs alike are drawn to this metal for the same reasons: superior durability and low maintenance. First employed for high-power cooking ranges, stainless steel later came to be used for dishwashers and refrigerators, then cabinets, backsplashes, and countertops. Chrome, which is similar in appearance to stainless steel but less expensive, can sometimes be found on appliances as well. Of course, this industrial-looking metal is also a common choice for faucets and cabinet hardware. The use of stainless steel and chrome is particularly appropriate in lofts, given the powerful presence and history of metal in these former industrial spaces. As a result, the style fits right in with the loft aesthetic.

Soon after homeowners became enchanted with the commercial look in their kitchens, they started to incorporate it into their baths. Today sinks, faucets, and such accessories as lighting and mirrors are readily available in stainless steel or chrome. Again, because of the connection between metal and industry, such fixtures and accoutrements seem especially at home in a loft. Many loft dwellers opt for sink

OPPOSITE: *Sunlight bounces off the maple cabinets and floor in this loft, projecting a sense of warmth. Stainless steel appliances provide contrast, while splashes of red inject a note of unpredictability.*

designs in which the plumbing is visible rather than hidden, thereby echoing the exposed ductwork and piping characteristic of the main living spaces.

Concrete often plays a starring role in loft kitchens and baths as well. Although its residential use was once limited to garages and home workshops, this raw-looking material can now be found in the performance spaces—and even living spaces—of the most sophisticated homes. Usually treated with a stain-resistant finish and sometimes even a blush of color, concrete—a composite of natural elements—is extremely durable, resembling stone in appearance. It can be used for counters and floors and even molded into sinks, tubs, and showers to achieve an industrial, but nonetheless stylish, look.

Other common materials for both the kitchen and bath include wood, stone, and glass. Again, because each of these could be found in factories, they fit perfectly into the modern-day incarnation of the loft. Countertops and flooring are often composed of these materials, and some fixtures, such as sinks, can be made of glass or stone.

When it comes to the layout of space, the loft kitchen tends to be open to the rest of the living areas, just as in the great room of a suburban home. The setup not only allows family members to spend more time together, playing into today's more casual lifestyle, but also makes the most of the loft's expansive floor plan.

When located off a bedroom, particularly the master bedroom, baths are often kept somewhat open as well. By leaving the tub, shower, and vanity exposed to the sleeping area, a bedroom suite can enjoy an open feel that mimics the sense of space in the rest of the loft. For most loft dwellers, only the commode requires a private stall. To accommodate guests, a small powder room can be built into a corner of the loft, intruding minimally on floor space.

Keeping the kitchen and bath exposed to adjacent areas presents a challenge to the integrity of a loft. The odds and ends of everyday life run the risk of being revealed, and such clutter threatens to compromise the clean, open feeling treasured in a loft.

To avoid that undesirable result, homeowners go to great lengths to conceal their personal matters. Many a loft kitchen features a work island, which not only provides extra surface space for meal preparation but also helps to create a boundary line between the cooking area and the rest of the loft. When the side of the island closest to the other living spaces features a breakfast bar that is higher than the work surface on the inside of the island, an effective shield is created, allowing kitchen clutter to remain out of sight. In both the kitchen and the bath, space-efficient storage is key. Streamlined cabinets and unobtrusive drawers hold items big and small, keeping them hidden. And when the mess is just too much to stow away—picture the kitchen after the preparation of a large dinner—a screen or panel can be pulled into place to temporarily mask the area.

OPPOSITE: *In this kitchen, the exposed metal legs of the island speak to the industrial flavor of loft design. Movable metal cabinets on wheels provide handy storage beneath the work surface. Off to the side, a "wall" of galvanized metal bins stores smaller accessories neatly out of sight. One row of shelving is left open to display a selection of attractive pieces, while a library ladder provides access to the uppermost shelves.*

LEFT: *A long counter and a slight change in floor level set this kitchen apart from the rest of the loft. To give guests and family members the opportunity to visit with the cook, sleek bar stools offer comfortable perches. A row of drawers under the counter stores napkins and other small items.*

ABOVE: *Faced completely in stainless steel, the base of the island fits right in with the commercial-style refrigerator and range hood. The gleaming metal surfaces offer pleasing contrast to the warm wood floor and surrounding wood cabinetry.*

LEFT: *A glimpse of the refrigerator is the only indication that a kitchen lies behind this L-shaped counter. A row of three schoolhouse lamps does hint at the space's work-oriented role, however.*

OPPOSITE: *A serving counter that is several inches taller than the work surface conceals the kitchen from the surrounding areas. To complement the spare design, the counters are left free of small appliances and other clutter.*

OPPOSITE: *Because glass makes up much of this bathroom, the occupants can enjoy plenty of natural light, as well as the view. In order to ensure some privacy, the lower portion of the glass wall overlooking the rest of the loft features opaque panels.*

RIGHT: *Minimalist in design, this concrete sink resembles an industrial washbasin. Floating shelves serve as an airy counterpoint to the sink's solid mass.*

ABOVE, LEFT: *In this bath, strategically placed windows allow in light without compromising privacy. A powerful geometry pervades the space, from the wall panels to the tiles on the floor and the tub surround.*

ABOVE, RIGHT: *A glass sink basin looks as though it's floating on air. The exposed chrome plumbing underneath gives the unit a look that is both industrial and chic. Since there is no counter, a wall-mounted accessory provides a place for the soap.*

ABOVE: *Sheathed almost entirely in concrete, this bath looks industrial and luxurious at the same time. The streamlined metal counter and graceful chrome faucet pick up the silvery gray tones of the walls.*

OPPOSITE: *A colorful round pod forms a bath en suite. Glass block invites in light and visually expands the compact space.*

RIGHT: *The tiles lining the lower portion of the shower tie in with the lively color scheme of the pod's exterior and the rest of the bedroom. Although the efficient space contains just the bare necessities, it certainly doesn't skimp on personality.*

ABOVE: *A series of frosted panels with colorful edges conceals an adjacent bath. Surrounded by a sea of white, the panels pack a playful punch in the otherwise tranquil bedroom.*

RIGHT: *Inside the bath, the sherbet hues of the panels stand out against the multitude of white surfaces. The curved tub enclosure is left open at the top, giving the bath and bedroom the feeling of a shared space without depriving either of privacy.*

CHAPTER FIVE

CREATING COMFORT

To make a loft truly habitable, far more is needed than distinct activity zones and strategic lighting. Like any home, a loft needs to serve as a relaxing sanctuary for its inhabitants. To achieve this goal, it must be outfitted with furnishings that not only perform such basic services as providing a place to sit or sleep, but also offer comfort and speak to the owners' aesthetic sensibilities.

Furnishing a loft requires careful planning. While homeowners must incorporate pieces that are necessary for living and perhaps working, they must do so in a manner that interferes as little as possible with both the vastness of the floor plan and the impressive architectural design of the overall space. For this reason, lofts are often furnished in a minimalist fashion.

Selecting furnishings for a loft can be difficult, as they need to work in harmony with the oversize scale of the space. Pieces that seem right at home in a traditional house or apartment can easily be dwarfed by the expansive floor plan and soaring architecture of a loft. To avoid this undesirable outcome, the majority of pieces should be chosen to complement the sprawling surroundings. This strategy gives homeowners the freedom to incorporate a large dining table that seats ten, twelve, or even fourteen—perfect for those who like to entertain. And an overstuffed armchair sized to accommodate two can certainly hold its own in a loft setting. For contrast or whimsy, many designers also include a smattering of more delicate pieces, such as a leggy telephone table or a spindly floor lamp.

As far as style goes, many loft dwellers consider the simple lines, industrial materials, and large scale of contemporary and modernist furnishings a perfect fit. Pieces by the masters of the mid–twentieth century—Ray and Charles Eames, Le Corbusier, and Mies van der Rohe, to name a few—appear frequently in today's lofts, as do reproductions and pieces inspired by the work of these designers. The synergy between lofts and these furnishings, particularly those of the modernists, is natural, as the evolutions of both were rooted in a movement toward open-plan living.

OPPOSITE: *Furnishing a loft need not be a serious affair. The lighthearted, whimsical air in this space proves that a well-orchestrated mix of color and pattern can have stylish results.*

Of course, loft dwellers are far too creative to limit themselves to midcentury-modern and contemporary furnishings. Designers often bring in a few more traditional pieces to serve as accents and provide an element of surprise. Some even consider the rich palette and extensive detailing of antique pieces to be the perfect complements to the brick walls and dark, battered wood floors of a loft.

To maintain the open feel that loft dwellers so cherish in their floor plans, many homeowners opt for built-in furniture when possible. Streamlined against walls, such furnishings intrude little on floor space. In a living area, built-in seating offers a seamless look, appearing to grow out of the surrounding architecture. And in the bedroom, built-in drawers and cabinets lining one wall can keep clothing and accessories out of sight in an orderly and unobtrusive fashion. A built-in floating shelf off to the side of a bed can serve as a nightstand while preserving the open, airy feel of the loft.

Some designs allow furnishings to be tucked out of the way when not needed. Murphy beds, for instance, fold up into the wall or cabinetry, where they are concealed by a panel between uses. Particularly convenient for a guest room that doubles as a study, Murphy beds perform their function without permanently usurping square footage. Similarly, a writing surface can be designed to fold into the wall when not in use, simply dropping into place with the flip of a latch. A clever designer may even incorporate storage in the wall behind the desk, creating space for files, office supplies, and even a computer monitor and tower.

Indeed, storage plays an important role in the design of a loft. To maintain the clean, open look, the flotsam and jetsam of everyday life must be carefully contained. Whether hidden in closets or tucked into a series of bins, excess clutter is kept out of sight. The most successfully designed storage pieces serve as architectural elements— visually appealing in their own right.

Equally important when designing a space are color and texture. Introduced into a room through not only furniture, but also artwork and floor coverings, these elements play into the overall appearance of a room and merit careful consideration. When incorporated with restraint, these finishing touches can have a powerful impact. Appropriate accents may include a coir rug, with its scratchy texture, or an oil painting featuring thick, heavy strokes.

While there are many aspects that come into play when furnishing a loft, paying close attention to these design considerations can result in stunning spaces. More importantly, the deft integration of these elements can help homeowners transform their lofts into places they are proud to call home.

OPPOSITE: *A neutral palette sets a serene mood in this space. The look is anything but bland, though, thanks to the interplay of textures—from the fibers of the rug and the wood grain of the floor to the burnish of the leather chair.*

ABOVE: *With their simple lines and unassuming forms, midcentury-modern furnishings are right at home in a loft. The low profile of the minimalist sofa allows the soaring dimensions of the space to take center stage.*

RIGHT: *An arm's reach away, the urban landscape becomes the wallpaper for this dining area. The selection of spare furnishings keeps attention focused on the view.*

OPPOSITE: *Though not common, a traditional touch can work well in a loft. Here, a timeworn coffee table and a plump sofa perfectly complement the rustic brick wall and aged wood floor.*

RIGHT: *Accessories in earthy colors and textures provide contrast to this loft's clean, pale backdrop. The overstuffed design of the sofa introduces a softening touch, as well.*

ABOVE: *Set against a blue backdrop, a row of four rush-seat chairs becomes a life-size art installation. The warmth of the wood juxtaposed against the cool hue of the wall provides pleasing contrast.*

ABOVE: *In this medley of styles, a traditional wood table, a set of no-nonsense chairs, and a fanciful chandelier make for a memorable setting. For those who entertain often, a surprising combination of elements such as this may be just the thing to intrigue and delight guests.*

LEFT: *In this loft, an abundance of curvy silhouettes contrasts with the sharp edges that are often unavoidable in renovated industrial spaces. From the modernist light fixture and dining set to the various pieces of artwork, the forms are soft and voluptuous.*

ABOVE: *A novel patchwork of sweaters, this quilt demands a closer look. The noteworthy bed covering, along with an assortment of furnishings in playful shapes and colors, reveals the homeowner's sense of humor.*

ABOVE: *In this home office, an L-shaped desk seems to melt into the adjacent wall. Meanwhile, a bank of file cabinets rests quietly below the windows, providing easy access to papers without obstructing the view. The overall setup is both streamlined and efficient.*

RIGHT: *Bedside tables, cantilevered to the wall, appear to float in midair. Contributing to the overall minimalist look, they perform their function without cluttering the space.*

ABOVE, LEFT: *In this loft entrance, a clever designer has transformed a mundane necessity into an artistic statement. Frosted glass panels serve as the "doors" of a closet, obscuring—but not blocking—the view of jackets and paraphernalia stored inside. Mounted on tracks, the panels slide from side to side for easy access.*

ABOVE, RIGHT: *This creative loft dweller missed no opportunity for eye-catching design. Instead of typical doors, a geometric play of panels conceals the closet. The metallic finish on the doors reflects the industrial history of the space.*

RIGHT: *A platform bed and a coordinating nightstand give this bedroom an appropriately modern look. Although uncluttered, the space does not seem stark, thanks to the piece of artwork, the billowy bed linens, and the deep-pile shag rug.*